KU-719-774

# What About Health?

# Drugs

by Fiona Waters

HODDER
Wayland

an imprint of Hodder Children's Books

# Titles in the WHAT ABOUT HEALTH? series

Drugs

Exercise

Food

Hygiene

**Drugs** is a simplified version of the title
**Drugs and Your Health** in Wayland's 'Health Matters' series.

Language level consultant: Norah Granger
Editor: Belinda Hollyer
Designer: Jane Hawkins

Text © 2001 Hodder Wayland
Volume © 2001 Hodder Wayland

First published in 2001 by Hodder Wayland,
an imprint of Hodder Children's Books.

British Library Cataloguing in Publication Data
Waters, Fiona
Drugs. - (What about health?)
1.Drugs - Physiological effect - juvenile literature
I.Title
615.7
ISBN 0 7502 3607 8

Printed in Hong Kong

Hodder Children's Books
A division of Hodder Headline Ltd
338 Euston Road, London NW1 3BH

Picture acknowledgements
Illustrations: Jan Sterling
Cover: Hodder Wayland Picture Library (except pills, Eye Ubiquitous);
Allsport 21(top); Format 23 (top right); Sally & Richard Greenhill Photo
Library 14; Hodder Wayland Picture Library 9;The Hutchison Library
28; Popperfoto 22 (bottom left); Science Photo Library 8 (both), 23
(centre left & right); South American Pictures 12; Tony Stone 4,
6, 7, 11, 15, 22 (right), 24, 26; Topham 13; Zefa Picture Library
10, 16, 19, 20, 21 (bottom), 23 (top left).

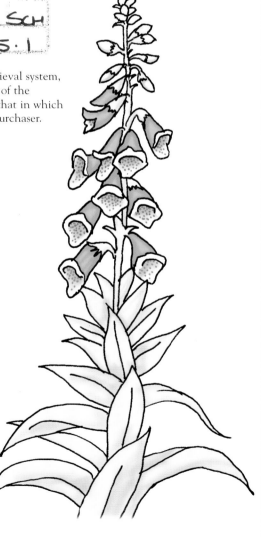

# Contents

# What are drugs?

Drugs can change the way our bodies and minds work. Some drugs can stop you getting ill. Some drugs can help your body get better. The drugs your doctor gives you help your body get back to normal.

Some drugs stop your body working properly. Tobacco and alcohol can be bad for your body. It is against the law to take some drugs. They are called illegal drugs. They can make you very ill. They can even kill you.

Medical drugs can help you get better after an illness. They can help you to get your energy back.
▼

There are hundreds of different kinds of drug. Some are tablets. Some are creams you have to rub on to your skin. Some are liquids that you have to drink. ▶

◀ Your age and size will affect the way drugs work on you.

Caffeine is a drug in tea, coffee and cola drinks. It is bad for you to drink too much caffeine. When you stop drinking it you may get headaches and feel bad tempered. ▶

# Drugs can make you feel better

Drugs that make you better or take away pain are called medicines. Some medicines help to make colds better, and some are painkillers. If you have an upset tummy you can take medicine. Antibiotics are drugs that kill germs in your body.

You can buy some medicines from the supermarket or the chemist shop. You need to visit the doctor for some others.

The doctor can check on a computer how much of a drug you need to make you better. The doctor will give you a prescription to take to the chemist.▼

Your body can fight some illnesses by itself. A cold can often get better if you just rest and drink lots of water. ▶

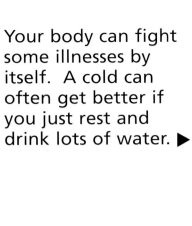

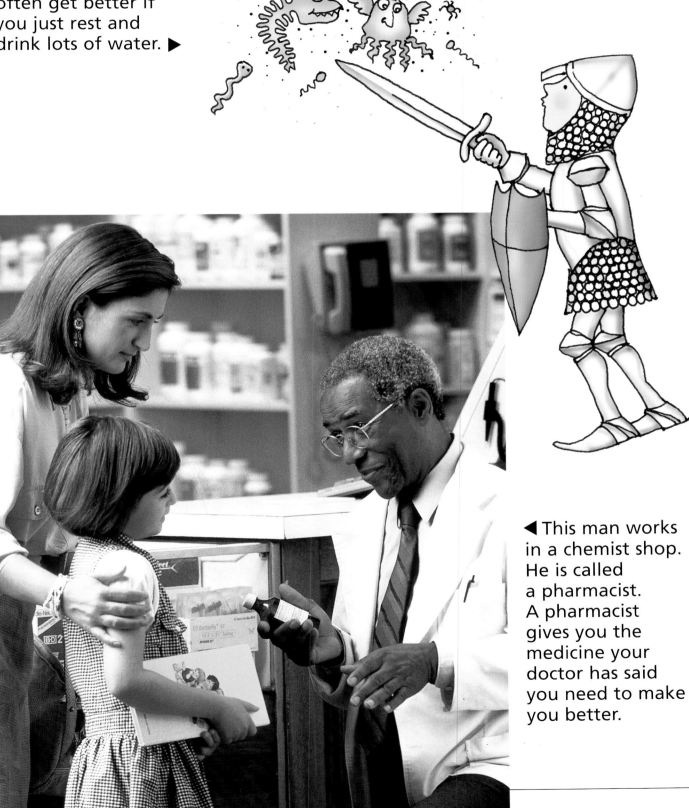

◀ This man works in a chemist shop. He is called a pharmacist. A pharmacist gives you the medicine your doctor has said you need to make you better.

# Longer life

Modern medicines help people to live much longer than they did in the past. But as you get older, you may become less fit. Drugs can help people stay alive and without pain.

Some people need to take drugs every day, to take pain away or to stay healthy.

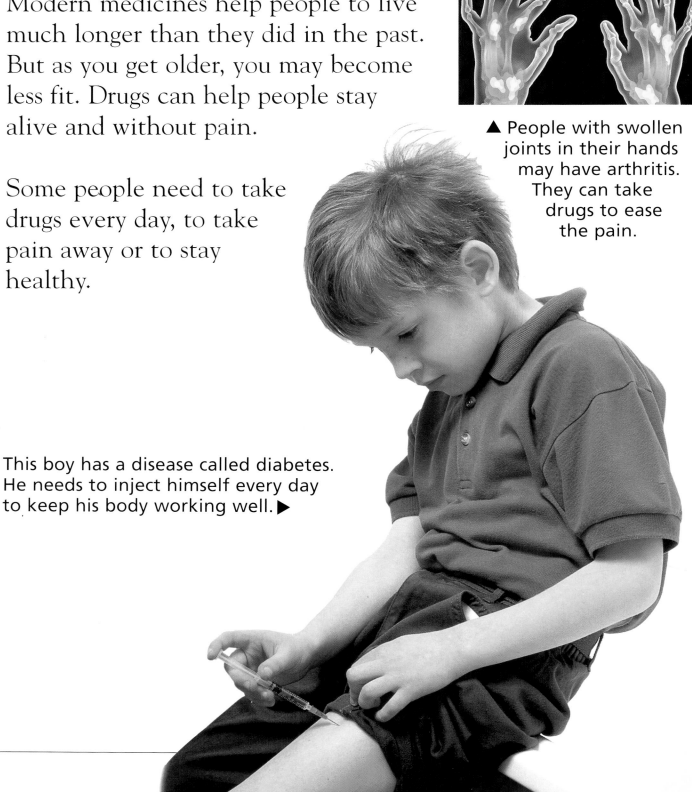

▲ People with swollen joints in their hands may have arthritis. They can take drugs to ease the pain.

This boy has a disease called diabetes. He needs to inject himself every day to keep his body working well. ▶

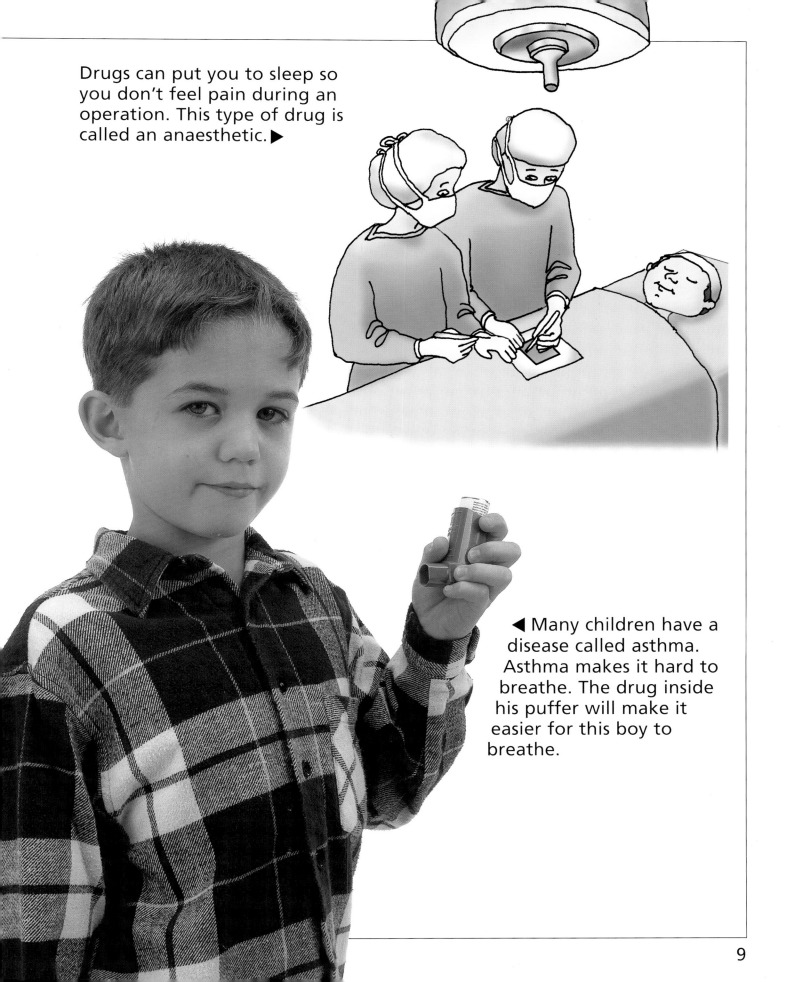

Drugs can put you to sleep so you don't feel pain during an operation. This type of drug is called an anaesthetic. ▶

◀ Many children have a disease called asthma. Asthma makes it hard to breathe. The drug inside his puffer will make it easier for this boy to breathe.

# How drugs are made

Drugs are made in buildings called laboratories. Drugs can be taken from plants or animals. They can also be made from chemicals. It can take years to find a new drug. Then the drug needs to be tested to make sure it is safe.

Scientists make models of new drugs on a computer screen. Then tests can be done on live animals like rats or mice.

Scientists try to find new drugs. They want to cure diseases like cancer and HIV. ▼

Many people do not like animals to be used for the tests. The scientists say they want to be sure the drug is safe to give to humans.

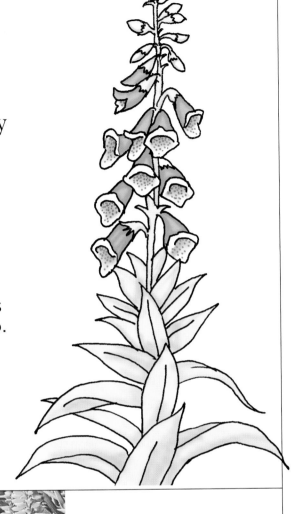

The first medicines came from plants hundreds and hundreds of years ago. A drug called digitalis comes from foxglove leaves. It is used to treat heart disease. ▶

You can find out some of the medicines that come from plants. Visit your local health shop and look at the labels on the bottles.

# Drugs in the past

People have used drugs for thousands of years.  People took drugs to feel better.  Sometimes they used drugs in their religious ceremonies.

People high in the mountains of South America used to chew coca leaves to help them work in the thin air.  Opium and cannabis were used in Asia to take away pain. The Aztecs in Mexico used to eat mushrooms which made them feel strange.

A woman sells coca leaves at a market in the mountains of Peru. Coca leaves contain cocaine.▼

In the 1920s, alcohol was banned in the United States. So people made their own alcohol illegally. ▶

▲ In the Second World War some pilots took drugs called amphetamines to keep them awake.

In the 1950s and 1960s some young people took drugs like cannabis. ▶

# How drugs work

Drugs come in many forms. Some are injected into your blood. You breathe some in through your nose. These drugs work very quickly. Others need to work very slowly.

Drugs can copy natural chemicals in your body. They can also stop these chemicals from working.

A syringe works like a bicycle pump. The medicine is pushed down into the needle by air pressure. ▼

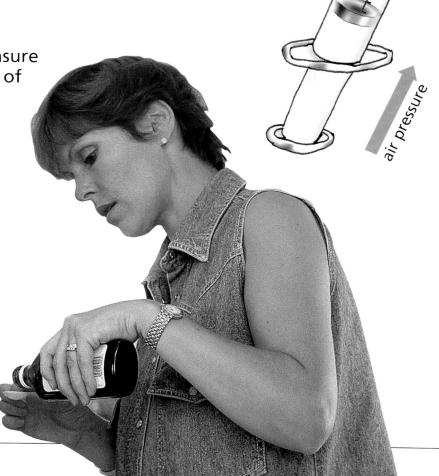

air pressure

It is important to measure out the right amount of medicine.▼

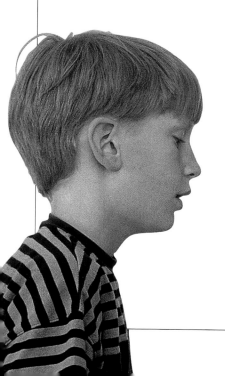

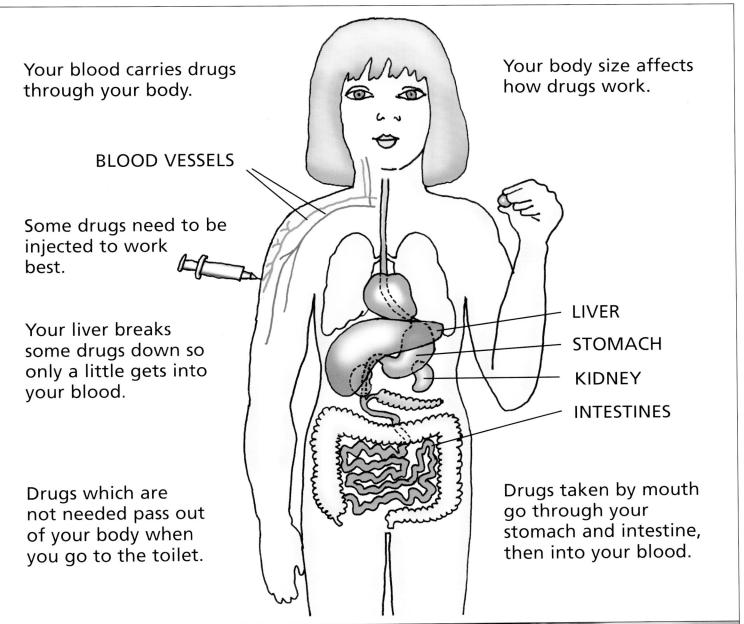

Your blood carries drugs through your body.

BLOOD VESSELS

Some drugs need to be injected to work best.

Your liver breaks some drugs down so only a little gets into your blood.

Drugs which are not needed pass out of your body when you go to the toilet.

Your body size affects how drugs work.

LIVER

STOMACH

KIDNEY

INTESTINES

Drugs taken by mouth go through your stomach and intestine, then into your blood.

Some medicines are made just for children. Can you find out how they are different from medicines for adults?

# Safety and drugs

All drugs can harm you if you do not use them properly. You should always read the labels. They tell you the right amounts to take. They tell you how often you need to take the drug. And they tell you if you need to take it before or after you eat.

▲You should keep drugs in a cool and dark place. Some medicines have a 'use by' date.

You should not take some drugs with alcohol. Milk can stop some antibiotics from working properly. Some drugs can make you sleepy.

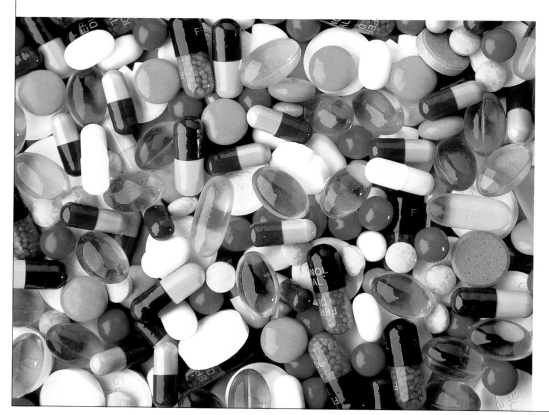

◀ Bright coloured tablets can look like sweets to young children. They should be kept in a safe place.

You should never take someone else's medicine, even if you have the same illness. ▶

The medicines in a first-aid cupboard must be kept safe. Can you think of ways to do that?

# Drinking and smoking

All over the world, many people smoke and drink alcohol. They say alcohol and tobacco make them feel better. Both are really drugs that can harm your body. More people die from the nicotine in tobacco smoke than from any other drug.

Alcohol and tobacco can harm, or even kill, an unborn baby.▶

When you breathe in someone else's smoke it is called passive smoking.▼

Many adults and young people drink alcohol.
A small amount can be good for people. But if
they drink too much, it will damage their
livers. Road accidents can be caused by
people who drive when they have been
drinking alcohol.

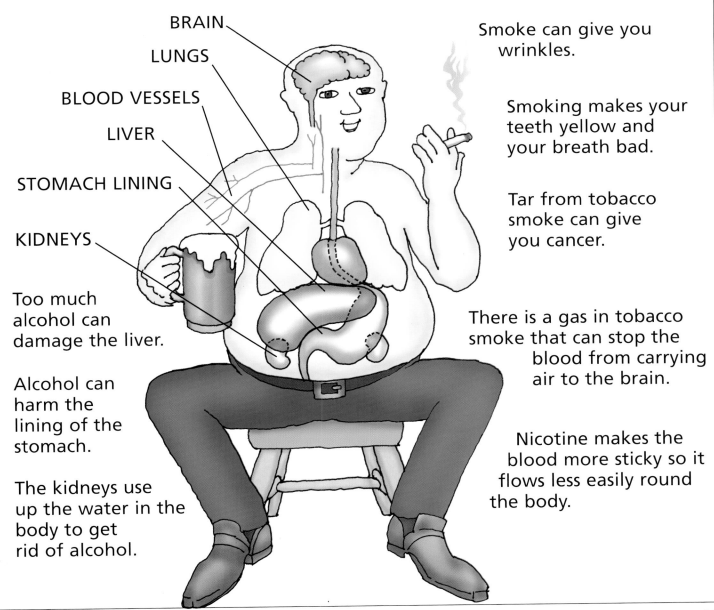

BRAIN

LUNGS

BLOOD VESSELS

LIVER

STOMACH LINING

KIDNEYS

Too much
alcohol can
damage the liver.

Alcohol can
harm the
lining of the
stomach.

The kidneys use
up the water in the
body to get
rid of alcohol.

Smoke can give you
wrinkles.

Smoking makes your
teeth yellow and
your breath bad.

Tar from tobacco
smoke can give
you cancer.

There is a gas in tobacco
smoke that can stop the
blood from carrying
air to the brain.

Nicotine makes the
blood more sticky so it
flows less easily round
the body.

# Drugs in sport

Sportspeople can use drugs to build muscles and give them energy. Some drugs can be used as medicine, but are not allowed to be used in sport. There are other drugs which are illegal.

Drugs pass out of the body in urine. Urine samples are taken from sportspeople after they have performed. If drugs are found in their samples, they may be banned for months. Sometimes they are banned for ever.

Some sportspeople take drugs to help them win. But many others think taking drugs is cheating.▼

Drugs called anabolic steroids build big muscles. They are banned from sports. ▼

▲ Some sportspeople will take illegal drugs to make them run faster. The drugs can be dangerous.

Tablets called beta-blockers can slow down the heart and calm nerves. ▼

◄ Painkillers will let a player play on after an injury.

# Illegal drugs

Illegal drugs can harm your mind and your body.
They can make you feel good at first, but they
can also make you feel very bad.

Illegal drugs can make you feel dizzy and strange.
They can make you see things that are not
really there.

Nine illegal drugs – from left to right:

Top row: heroin, ecstasy (E), cannabis

Middle row: magic mushroom, acid
(LSD), cannabis

Bottom row: cocaine, crack, speed ▶

 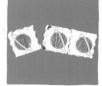 

◀ Some people take ecstasy
(E) in clubs to give them
more energy. People have
died from taking it.

▲ Cocaine and crack speed up the heart and give energy. But they can also cause panic and terrible anxiety.

▲ Amphetamines give energy. But they also make it hard to eat and sleep.

Acid (LSD) makes people feel very odd. They can see strange pictures in their heads. ▶

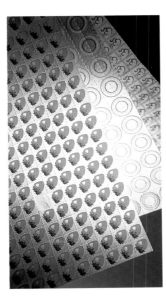

◀ Cannabis can make people feel relaxed. But smoking it can cause lung cancer.

◀ Glue and lighter fuel have a very strong smell. Some people sniff or spray them into their mouths. The chemicals in them can kill you.

# Addictive drugs

Addiction is when the mind and body start to need more and more of a drug. Alcohol and nicotine are addictive drugs. So are cocaine and heroin.

People who are addicted to drugs are called drug addicts. Often, they can't think of anything except getting more drugs. At first the drugs make them feel good, but then they can't stop. They may steal because they need money to buy more drugs.

◄ A baby whose mother is a drug addict will be born addicted too.

# THE EFFECTS ON THE BODY OF TAKING ECSTASY (E)

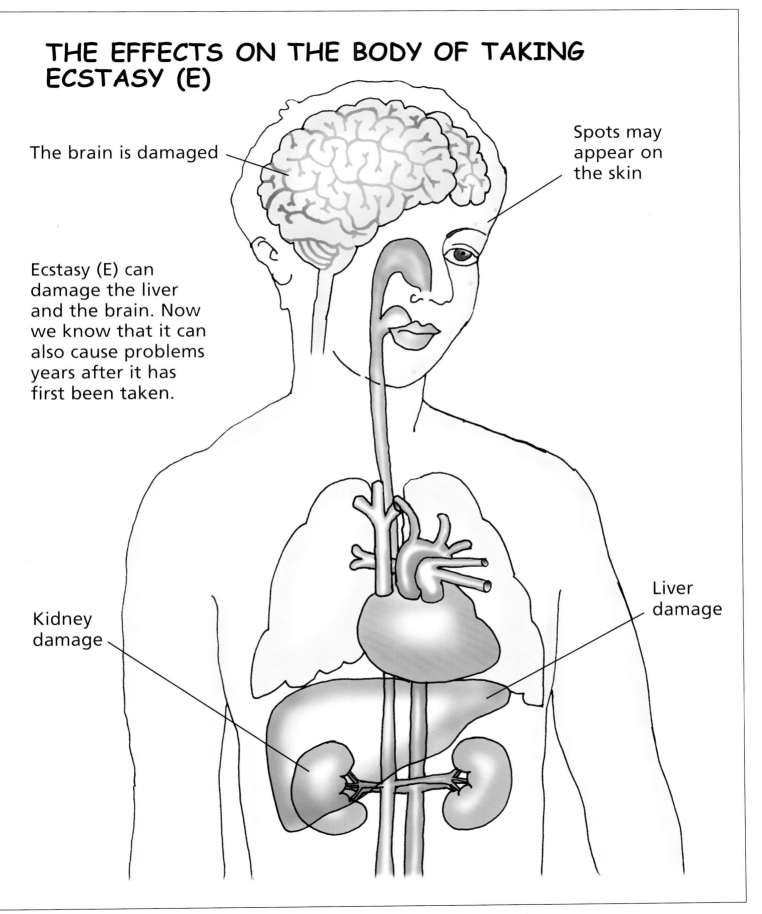

The brain is damaged

Spots may appear on the skin

Ecstasy (E) can damage the liver and the brain. Now we know that it can also cause problems years after it has first been taken.

Kidney damage

Liver damage

# Problems with drugs

Illegal drugs cause a great many problems. People get sick and die from taking illegal drugs. People who sell illegal drugs are called drug dealers. If dealers are caught, they are sent to prison.

A sniffer dog looks for hidden drugs on a plane.▼

Most countries have laws about drugs. In Britain, the United States and Australia it is illegal to buy or sell cocaine or heroin. Alcohol is also illegal in some countries.

Customs officers at ports and airports try to stop people bringing in illegal drugs. They use specially trained sniffer dogs who can hunt for the drugs by smell.

◀ Illegal drugs can be hidden in flour or talcum powder. Sometimes tablets sold as drugs are actually ordinary aspirins.

## WHY DO PEOPLE TAKE ILLEGAL DRUGS?

- To feel good
- To try to look 'cool'
- To relax
- To escape from the real world

# The good and the bad

The drugs given to you by your doctor or bought at the chemist are good for you. They will make you feel better. They are very carefully tested before they are given to people.

Illegal drugs can make you very sick indeed. They can harm your body and your mind. They may make you feel good, but not for long.

Swimming is fun and makes you feel good. It is also good for your body. ▼

Dancing and swimming and running can all make you feel good. They also help to keep your body fit.

If you want to feel dizzy, try cartwheels and somersaults. ▶

▲ You do not need drugs to see pictures in your head. You can make your own pictures if you close your eyes.

It can be hard to say 'no' if you are offered illegal drugs. But saying 'no' means that you are strong. Learning to keep safe is part of growing up.

# Glossary

**Addictive**  A drug that makes you want it all the time.

**Amphetamines**  Tablets that make you feel excited and wide awake.

**Anabolic steroids**  Drugs that build muscles.

**Anaesthetic**  A drug that takes away pain. Some anaesthetics put you to sleep.

**Antibiotics**  Drugs that can kill bacteria in your body.

**Arthritis**  A very painful disease that makes joints swell.

**Asthma**  An illness that makes it very hard to breathe.

**Beta-blockers**  Drugs that are used to slow down the heart rate.

**Caffeine**  A natural drug that is found in coffee, tea, chocolate and cola drinks.

**Diabetes**  A disease that makes it difficult for the body to make its own sugar.

**HIV**  One of the viruses that can cause a serious illness called AIDS.

**Intestine**  The long tube that takes waste from your stomach.

**Nicotine**  A natural drug that is found in tobacco smoke.

# Finding out more

## BOOKS TO READ

*Drugs and Medicine* by Jenny Bryan   (Wayland, 1992)

*The Don't Spoil Your Body Book*   by Claire Rayner  (Bodley Head, 1989)

*What do You Know About Drugs?*   by Pete Sanders and Steve Myers (Aladdin, 1995)

## ORGANIZATIONS

The National Drugs Helpline
Freephone  0800 776600

Institute for the Study of Drug Dependence
32 Loman Street
London SE1 0EE

# Index